CHILD CARE LAW

A SUMMARY

NORTHERN IRELAND

Michael Long

BAAF
ADOPTION
& FOSTERING

Published by
British Association for Adoption & Fostering
(BAAF)
Saffron House
6–10 Kirby Street
London EC1N 8TS
www.baaf.org.uk

Charity registration 275689 (England and Wales) and SC039337 (Scotland)

© Michael Long, 2014

British Library Cataloguing in Publication Data
A catalogue record for this book is available from the British Library

ISBN 978 1 907585 87 6

Designed and typeset by Helen Joubert Design

Printed in Great Britain by TJ International

Trade distribution by Turnaround Publisher Services, Unit 3, Olympia Trading Estate, Coburg Road, London N22 6TZ

BAAF is the leading UK-wide membership organisation for all those concerned with adoption, fostering and child care issues.

Contents

Note about the author

Michael Long was called to the Bar of Northern Ireland in 1975. He took silk in September 1996 (which, fortuitously, coincided with the coming into force of the Children (Northern Ireland) Order 1995). He specialises in family law and appeared for the child in the Court of Appeal and House of Lords in *H & R v Down Lisburn CH&SST*. He is the author of *The Law of Adoption in Northern Ireland* and *Human Rights, Freeing and Contact* and the co-author of *The Law of Children in Northern Ireland*. He was the Bar representative on the Departmental working group on the reform of adoption law and was the primary author of the *Guide to Case Management in Public Law Proceedings* (2009) and the *Guide to Case Management in Private Law Proceedings* (2013). He is a member of the Family Proceedings Rules Committee.

Acknowledgements

I found the companion work to this for England and Wales, *Child Care Law: A summary of the law in England and Wales*, now in its fifth edition, by Deborah Cullen and Mary Lane, most useful both in indicating what was required and as a check that I had not left anything out. Thanks also to Siobhan Keegan QC and Kathryn Stevenson for reviewing the text, and in Kathryn's case providing information on leaving care and other improvements to the text. I am grateful to all those at BAAF, particularly its publisher, Shaila Shah, for commissioning this work and putting it together in the excellent format which you will find, and, as ever, to my wife Margaret Walsh QC.

Introduction

This short book contains a summary of the main legal provisions and principles affecting the law relating to child care in Northern Ireland. It provides a general overview and an introduction for those who want to learn more. Of necessity, it contains many generalisations and simplifications, and consequently it does not provide legal advice. All cases involving children are fact-sensitive and those involved in such cases ought to seek proper independent legal advice at the earliest stage.

Terms used in this book

- In general terms, a **child** is a person under 18.

- The main legislative provisions governing child care in Northern Ireland are the **Children (Northern Ireland) Order 1995** and the **Adoption (Northern Ireland) Order 1987**. The latter is subject to review at the time of writing (summer 2013) and may be replaced in the next few years.

- The term **"public law proceedings"** is a generic term embracing all those proceedings in which a public authority seeks an order in respect of a child, including any subsequent proceedings to vary or discharge such an order.

- **"Private law proceedings"** refers to proceedings in which the main parties are private individuals, usually – but not always – the child's parents.

- In Northern Ireland, the main public bodies involved are the five **Health and Social Care Trusts** referred to in this book and in common usage as **"the Trust"**.

- **"NIGALA"** is the **Northern Ireland Guardian ad Litem Agency**, which provides independent advice and representation for children in public law proceedings.

- **"ADR"** stands for **Alternative Dispute Resolution**, such as conciliation, mediation or arbitration.

- Nearly all proceedings commence in the Family Proceedings Court, from which some may be transferred to the Family Care Centre, from which some may be transferred to the Family Division of the High Court. Appeals by way of rehearing lie from the Family Proceedings Court to the Family Care Centre. Appeals from the Family Care Centre lie to the High Court. Such appeals are usually confined to points of law, although the High Court may allow a rehearing. Appeal from the High Court is limited to points of law only and lies to the Court of Appeal, and thence, with permission, to the Supreme Court.

- The law is always subject to change both by means of the legislative process and by courts interpreting legislative provision.

- *The Children Order Advisory Committee Best Practice Guidance*, the *Guide to Case Management in Private Law Proceedings*, the *Guide to Case Management in Public Law Proceedings*, all written decisions of the High Court and Court of Appeal, as well as court listings, are available at www. courtsni.gov.uk.

Sources of law

The basis of the ability of the State to regulate and decide issues relating to children in Northern Ireland is the duty of the monarch as *parens patriae* to take care of children[1] who, by definition, were not of an ability to look after themselves. The duty was exercisable in respect of children by wardship; historically, this was exercised by way of the inherent jurisdiction of the High Court, although it has become regulated by statute and powers have been conferred on other courts. The inherent jurisdiction of the High Court still exists today but only in relation to issues which are not otherwise provided for by statute. Although the jurisdiction is now much restricted, the principles of wardship – of acting in the best interests of the child, and of the court itself making inquiries to decide what is best for the child rather than simply relying on the information that the parties decide to place before it – still permeate family litigation in respect of children.

The sources of statute law in Northern Ireland are:

- **Acts of the Parliament of the United Kingdom**;

- **Statutory Instruments** made under those Acts ("SIs");

- **Acts of the Northern Ireland Legislative Assembly and Orders in Council** made during periods of direct rule which are equivalent to such Acts;

- **Statutory Rules and Orders** made under those Acts ("SR&Os");

- **Regulations of the European Union**;

- **International Treaties given direct effect by Act of Parliament**;

1   A child is a person under the age of 18 for most purposes (Article 2(2) of the Children Order).

- **International Treaties** that do not have direct effect but which establish general standards of international law to which regard is paid in interpreting and applying other statutory provisions.

- In addition, there is **extra-statutory guidance** as to the conduct of family proceedings.

The core Statutory Provisions

The main statutes relating to children are listed below.

- **The Children (Northern Ireland) Order 1995**, which regulates most private and public law proceedings in relation to child care. It is very similar to the Children Act 1989 applicable to England and Wales (in its original form).

- **The Adoption (Northern Ireland) Order 1987**, which is similar to the former Adoption Act 1976 in England and Wales.

(Both the Children (Northern Ireland) Order 1995 and the Adoption (Northern Ireland) Order 1987 are Orders in Council equivalent to Acts of the Assembly.

- **The Adoption Agencies Regulations (Northern Ireland) 1989**, which make provision for implementation of the Adoption Order.

- **The Child Abduction and Custody Act 1985**, an Act of Parliament applying throughout the United Kingdom, which incorporates into domestic law the Hague Convention on the Civil Aspects of International Child Abduction.

- **The Family Law Act 1986**, an Act of Parliament applying throughout the United Kingdom, which regulates and allocates most proceedings relating to children between the various jurisdictions of the United Kingdom.

- **Council Regulation (EC) No. 2201/2003**, a Regulation of the Council of the European Union (commonly known as "Brussels IIb"), which regulates and allocates most family law proceedings between the various States of the European Union. It also provides for mutual recognition and enforcement of judgments. It is supplemented by Guidance Notes. It has direct application.

- **The Hague Convention on the Protection of Children 1996**, which has a similar object in relation to some proceedings relating to children as Brussels IIb. It is directly applicable, being treated as an EC treaty, but Brussels IIb takes precedence where it applies. There have only been a limited number of signatories.

- **The European Convention on Human Rights and Fundamental Freedoms**, most of the provisions of which have direct application by virtue of the provisions of The Human Rights Act 1998, and Act of Parliament applying throughout the United Kingdom.

- **The United Nations Convention on the Rights of the Child 1989**, which does not have direct application but is to be used as an aid to interpretation of the European Convention on Human Rights and Fundamental Freedoms.[2]

- **The Adoption (Intercountry Aspects) Act (Northern Ireland) 2001**, an Act of the Northern Ireland Assembly (which amended the Adoption (Northern Ireland) Order 1987), the Adoption of Children from Overseas Regulations (Northern Ireland) 2002 and the Intercountry Adoption (Hague Convention) Regulations (Northern Ireland) 2003, which make provision for the implementation in Northern Ireland of the Convention on Protection of Children and Co-Operation in respect of Intercountry Adoption 1993 and provide for the adoption of children from overseas in Northern Ireland and the adoption of children from Northern Ireland in other countries.

- **The Rules**. Court proceedings are regulated by rules made by the appropriate rule-making body, which rank as SR&Os. The relevant rules are **The Magistrates' Courts (Children (Northern Ireland) Order 1995) Rules (Northern Ireland) 1996**, which apply to proceedings in the Family Proceedings Court, and **The Family Proceedings Rules (Northern Ireland) 1996**, which apply to proceedings in the High Court and the Family Care Centre. Both are subject to the general rules of court applying to

---

2 See *Neulinger & Shuruk v Switzerland* [2011] 1 FLR 122 and *ZH (Tanzania) v Secretary of State for the Home Department* [2011] UKSC 4.

the relevant level of court. Both are supplemented by extra-statutory guidance, namely:

- **The Children Order Advisory Committee's Best Practice Guide (2nd edition)**
- **The Guide to Case Management in Public Law Proceedings**
- **The Guide to Case Management in Private Law Proceedings**

● The allocation of proceedings is specified in **The Children (Allocation of Proceedings) Order (Northern Ireland) 1996**, in respect of the implementation of which guidance as to the appropriate court which should hear proceedings is provided in the **Allocation of Family Proceedings – Notes for Guidance** (appended to the **Guide to Case Management in Public Law Proceedings**, but which applies to both public and private law proceedings).

Other regulations

The implementation of the Children Order is affected by various other regulations, the chief of which are listed below.

● **The Children (Admissibility of Hearsay Evidence) Order (Northern Ireland) 1996**, which provides for hearsay evidence to be admissible in connection with the upbringing, maintenance or welfare of a child.

● **The Children (Parental Responsibility Agreement) Regulations (Northern Ireland) 1996**, which makes provision for the form and registration of a parental responsibility agreement whereby a father who does not have parental responsibility may acquire it by agreement with the mother.

● **The Contact with Children Regulations (Northern Ireland) 1996**, which makes provision in relation to contact with children in care.

● **The Representations Procedure (Children) Regulations (Northern Ireland) 1996**, which sets out the procedure to be followed in relation to complaints about the discharge of an authority's functions under Part IV of the Children Order.

● **The Children (Private Arrangements for Fostering) Regulations**

(Northern Ireland) 1996, which regulate the discharge of an authority's functions under the Children Order in relation to children who are privately fostered.

- **The Arrangements for Placement of Children (General) Regulations (Northern Ireland) 1996,** which relate to the placement of a child in the care of an authority or voluntary organisation.

- **The Review of Children's Cases Regulations (Northern Ireland) 1996,** which provide for the initial and then periodic review by the relevant authority of the case of each child in the authority's care.

- **The Placement of Children with Parents Regulations (Northern Ireland) 1996**, which provide for the placement with parents of a child in the care of an authority.

- **The Foster Placement (Children) Regulations (Northern Ireland) 1996,** which provide for the approval of foster carers and regulate the placement of children in the care of an authority with foster carers.

- **The Children (Secure Accommodation) Regulations (Northern Ireland) 1996**, which make provision for the placement of certain children in secure accommodation.

Precedent

In all common law countries, courts rely on precedent, i.e. they follow earlier decisions of the same or higher courts so as to achieve consistency and certainty. The purpose of examining precedents is to identify principle. It is a pointless and fruitless exercise to seek to identify an earlier case which is exactly the same on the facts as the present case under consideration, as no two cases are ever exactly the same, and this is especially the case in family law.

Courts in Northern Ireland accord due deference to decisions of the High Court and Court of Appeal in England and Wales but are not bound by them.[3]

---

3   *McCartan v Belfast Harbour Commissioners* [1910] 2 IR 470 and *SH v RD & RH* [2012] NIFam 2.

Courts in Northern Ireland are bound by decisions of the Supreme Court on appeal from the Court of Appeal in Northern Ireland or on appeal from other courts within the UK where the law is the same or similar in both jurisdictions.

2

Human rights

The Human Rights Act 1998 brought into force throughout the UK most of the provisions of the European Convention on Human Rights and Fundamental Freedoms. It is unlawful for a public authority (which includes any court) to act in a way which is incompatible with a Convention right unless so required by one or more provisions of, or made under, primary legislation.

In some circumstances, it is possible to challenge the compatibility of legislation with the provisions of the Convention, but the result of such a challenge is a declaration of incompatibility which does not, in itself, change a legislative provision. Changing a legislative provision is a matter for the appropriate legislative body, not the court – but the court can require the relevant government department to provide guidelines in place of statutory provisions that have been found to be incompatible with the Convention.

Any court determining any question that has arisen in relation to a Convention right has to have regard to any judgement, decision, declaration or advisory opinion of the European Court of Human Rights, any opinion of the Commission adopted under Article 31 of the Convention, any decision of the Commission in connection with Articles 26 or 27(2) of the Convention, or any decision of the Committee of Ministers under Article 46 of the Convention.

Where a breach has taken place or an action has been proposed that would constitute a breach by a public authority, a relevant court may grant such relief as lies within its powers (usually quashing or prohibiting the impugned decision), but it can also make a declaration that a provision is incompatible with the terms of the Convention.

The provisions of the Convention most likely to be encountered in relation to family law are **Articles 5, 6 and 8**.

- **Article 5** provides for the right to liberty and security of person. No one can be deprived of that right except in certain specified cases and in accordance with a procedure prescribed by law. The excepted cases include detention of a minor by lawful order for the purpose of educational supervision, for the purpose of bringing him before the competent legal authority.

- **Article 6** provides for the right to a fair trial in the determination of civil rights and obligations or of any criminal charge against him by way of a fair and public hearing within a reasonable period of time by an independent and impartial tribunal established by law. Judgment is to be pronounced publicly but the press and public may be excluded from the trial in a number of circumstances, including 'where the interests of juvenile or the protection of the private life of the parties so require'.

- **Article 8** provides:
  1. *Everyone has the right to respect for his private and family life, his home and his correspondence.*
  2. *There shall be no interference by a public authority with the exercise of this right except such as in accordance with the interests of national security, public safety or the economic well-being of the country, for the prevention of disorder or crime, for the protection of health or morals, or for the protection of the rights and freedoms of others.*

Since the court is a public authority for the purposes of the Act, it follows that there is no area of family litigation involving children in which Articles 6 and 8 will have no application. In practical terms, Article 6 requires the parties to be at 'equality of arms', so that, for example, a private person should not be at a disadvantage in comparison to a public authority with greater financial resources. Article 8 has a multiplicity of applications but, in essence, any interference in the right to private life has to be proportionate, must be in pursuit of one of the legitimate aims specified in the Article, and must be necessary in a democratic society, which means that it must meet a pressing social need.

Thus, it has been held that the provisions of the Adoption Order preventing unmarried couples and same-sex couples from jointly adopting a child are incompatible with the provisions of the Convention, and a Health and Social Care Trust has been prevented from receiving back into Northern Ireland two children, the subject of care orders, who had been unlawfully abducted from Northern Ireland by their parents to the Republic of Ireland where they could be assessed in their new home without being brought back.

3

Jurisdiction

The physical presence of the child in Northern Ireland is always sufficient to enable emergency or protective steps to be taken until issues as to jurisdiction are resolved.

In all other cases, the issue of jurisdiction is likely to involve a consideration of the issue of in which jurisdiction the child is **habitually resident**.

Habitual residence

"Habitual residence", at least initially, has to be interpreted in the context of the Brussels IIb Regulations and the consequent European case law, and that interpretation may differ from the domestic interpretation of that term.

- **In European jurisprudence**, the term "habitual residence" involves a consideration of the context of the Regulations and a consideration of the integration of the child in a social and family environment. There must be physical presence but also a consideration of a wide range of factors such as nationality, linguistic ability, attendance at school, family and social relationships, and the reasons why the child is present in the jurisdiction. The joint intentions of those with parental responsibility have to be considered, as well as the steps taken by them to give effect to those intentions, such as the provision of housing, purchase of property and finding of employment.[1]

- **In domestic law**, "habitual residence" has been held to mean the voluntary assumption of a place of residence for settled purposes as a part of the

---

1   For example, *Re A (Area of Freedom, Security and Justice)* [2009] 2 FLR 1.

regular order of life, for the time being, whether of short or long duration.[2] The area of tension appears to relate to the degree of permanence and integration to be sought. The recent tendency in England and Wales has been to try to merge the definitions,[3] although there is no recent appellate authority in Northern Ireland on the issue.

It is obvious that the habitual residence of a child will depend much on that of his or her parent(s). Where parental responsibility is shared, habitual residence cannot be changed by the unilateral action of one parent alone.

Brussels IIb

Brussels IIb consists of a series of rules regulating which State of the European Union has jurisdiction to deal with proceedings concerning divorce, legal separation and marriage annulment, and parental responsibility for children and for the mutual recognition, registration and enforcement of judgments. Where it applies, it takes precedence over the provisions of the 1996 Hague Convention. That Convention has similar objects and many of the States of the EU are parties to it but other States outside the EU (for example, Australia) are also parties.

Brussels IIB and the 1996 Hague Convention both take precedence over the provisions of the Family Law Act 1986, which, where the Regulations and the Convention do not take effect, deals with the co-ordination of jurisdiction between the relevant courts of the various parts of the UK.

There are also various bilateral protocols between the UK and other countries (notably Egypt and Pakistan) that are not members of the EU or signatories to relevant international conventions, relating to issues of jurisdiction and enforcement.

2   *R v Barnet LBC ex p. Nilish Shah.*
3   See, for example, *Re H-K (Habitual Residence)* [2012] 1 FLR 436.

Parenting responsibility for children: who has jurisdiction?

In relation to parental responsibility for children, the general rule is that the courts of a member state have jurisdiction in relation to any child who is habitually resident in that member state (Article 8 of Brussels IIb), at the date on which the court is seised of the relevant application. However, this is subject to a number of exceptions:

a) where a child moves lawfully from one member state to another, the courts of the former retain jurisdiction for a period of three months after the move, unless the parties accept the jurisdiction of the latter (Article 9);

b) in the case of wrongful abduction or retention, the courts of the original place of habitual residence retain jurisdiction until the child has acquired habitual residence in the new country and either each person having rights of custody has acquiesced in the removal or retention, or the child has resided in the new country for at least a year after the person with rights of custody had, or should have had, knowledge of the child's presence there, and the child is settled there and either no request for return has been made, or any such request has been withdrawn or a case in the courts of the original member state has been closed or a judgment on custody has been made in those courts that does not require return (Article 10);

c) where an issue as to parental responsibility arises in connection with proceedings for divorce, legal separation or annulment and at least one of the spouses has parental responsibility and the jurisdiction has been accepted, then the courts of the member state in which the proceedings are pending has jurisdiction but the jurisdiction terminates when the proceedings terminate (Articles 12(1) and (2));

d) by agreement of the parties, the courts of a member state with which the child has a substantial connection may have jurisdiction (Article 12(3));

e) where the child has his or her habitual residence in a country outside the EU that is not a signatory to the 1996 Convention and it is found impossible to bring proceedings in that country, then jurisdiction may be deemed to be in the child's interests and may be exercised by the courts of the member state in which he or she is present (Article 12(4)).

If habitual residence cannot be determined, then physical presence confers jurisdiction (Article 13). The fall-back position beyond this is that domestic law as to jurisdiction applies (Article 14).

Courts should co-operate to determine which court is in a better position to determine issues of parental responsibility, and to that end a court properly seised of a matter can stay proceedings if it thinks that the courts of another member state are in a better position to deal with the matter. That can be done either on the application of a party or of a court in another member state, but at least one party to the proceedings has to agree and the child has to have a particular connection to the member state to which jurisdiction is to be ceded (Article 15).

In general, a court is seised when a document instituting the proceedings is lodged, provided that the applicant has not subsequently failed to take the steps which he or she is required to take in relation to service (Article 16).

The 1996 Hague Convention

Jurisdiction under the 1996 Convention is primarily based on **habitual residence**, and that term is presumably to be construed in accordance with domestic law. However, the **presence of property of a child** can also give rise to jurisdiction.

- Physical presence suffices in the cases of refugee children and children who are internationally displaced due to disturbances in their own country (Article 6).

- Exceptionally, physical presence enables courts of a country in which a child is not habitually resident to take emergency protection measures, but such measures only remain in force until the authorities of the country of habitual residence have taken the measures required in the situation (Article 11).

- In the case of a wrongful abduction or retention, the courts of the country of habitual residence retain jurisdiction (Article 7), but it can request the court of another country to accept jurisdiction if the child is a national of that country, or if property of the child is located in that country, or if the courts of that country are seised of an application for divorce, legal separation or marriage annulment of the child's parents, or if the child has a substantial connection with that country (Article 8).

- Similarly, such a country may request the court of the state of habitual residence to cede jurisdiction on the basis that the first country is in a better position to assess the child's best interests, but such cession cannot take place without the consent of the court of the state of habitual residence (Article 9).

- The Convention provides for courts to apply their own law but, exceptionally, they can apply or take into account the law of another State with which the situation has a substantial connection where that is necessary for the protection of the person or property of the child (Article 15).

In relation to parental responsibility, the Convention draws a distinction between attribution and exercise. In very general terms, parental responsibility is attributed by the law of the State of habitual residence. If a child changes habitual residence, parental responsibility is not extinguished by the move but it may be attributed to another person in accordance with the law of the new State of habitual residence. If a child moves, the exercise of parental responsibility depends on the law of the new State of habitual residence (Chapter 3 of the Convention).

The Family Law Act 1986

The Family Law Act 1986 only applies if the Regulations or the Convention do not. It relates to the attribution of jurisdiction in relation to orders of the type specified in Section 1 which are, in effect, Article 8 orders and orders under the inherent jurisdiction. Such orders are known in the Act as **"Part 1 orders"**.

A court in Northern Ireland can make Article 8 orders in respect of a child in matrimonial or civil partnership proceedings properly continuing in

Northern Ireland, but it cannot make such an order after making a decree of judicial separation proceedings for divorce, nullity, dissolution or annulment if proceedings are continuing in England and Wales or Scotland unless, in effect, the other court has ceded jurisdiction (Section 19A).

A court in Northern Ireland can make an Article 8 order separate from matrimonial proceedings if the child is habitually resident in Northern Ireland or if the child is physically present in Northern Ireland and is not habitually resident in any other part of the UK or a specified dependant territory, provided that matrimonial or civil partnership proceedings are not continuing in England and Wales, Scotland or a specified dependent territory unless, in effect, the other court has ceded jurisdiction (Section 20).

Even where proceedings are properly before a court in Northern Ireland, it has the power to stay proceedings if proceedings are continuing outside Northern Ireland and it seems more appropriate that the issues be determined in those proceedings. Such a stay can be removed in the event of unreasonable delay (Section 22). The Act also makes provision for the recognition, registration and enforcement of orders made elsewhere.

Forum conveniens

If neither the Regulations, nor the Convention, nor the Family Law Act apply, the court in Northern Ireland will limit its exercise of authority to temporary protective measures designed to ensure the return of the child to his or her own country if there are legal procedures in place in that country to achieve a fair hearing of competing parental claims.[4] If proceedings were brought in Northern Ireland, they would be stayed on the application of the party seeking to rely on another jurisdiction (the onus being on that party) if it were shown that another forum was the natural and appropriate forum, particularly in relation to convenience, expense and the availability of witnesses, and that the case had a substantial connection with that other country. The best interests of the child would be an important factor but not necessarily paramount.

4   *Re M (Jurisdiction: Forum Conveniens)* [1995] 2 FLR 224.

4

Principles applying to all Children Order cases

General principles

In every case in which a court is to determine any question with respect to the upbringing of a child or the administration of a child's property or any income arising from it, the child's welfare is the court's paramount consideration (Article 3(1) of the Children Order). "Paramount" means that welfare 'rules on and determines the course to be followed'.[1] In any proceedings in which any question with respect to the upbringing of a child arises, the court has to have regard for the general principle that any delay in determining the question is likely to prejudice the welfare of the child (Article 3(2)). If the court is considering the making, variation or discharge of an order under Article 8 of the Children Order, or a public law order, or the making of a parental responsibility order, it has to consider the "welfare checklist" set out in Article 3(3) of the Children Order (Article 3(4)) and a court should not make an order under the Children Order unless it considers that doing so would be better for the child than making no order at all (Article 3(5)).

The welfare checklist

The welfare checklist requires the court to have regard in particular to:

---

1   As per Lord McDermott in *J v C* [1970] AC 668.

a) the ascertainable wishes and feelings of the child concerned (considered in the light of his age and understanding);[2]

b) his physical, emotional and educational needs;

c) the likely effect on him of any change in his circumstances;

d) his age, sex, background and any characteristics of his which the court considers relevant;

e) any harm which he has suffered or is at risk of suffering;

f) how capable of meeting his needs is each of his parents and any other person in relation to whom the court considers the question to be relevant;

g) the range of powers available to the court under the Children Order in the proceedings in question.

Confidentiality

Proceedings concerning children are held in private so as to protect the children concerned. Consequently, it is an offence to publish any material that is likely to identify any child involved in proceedings under the Children Order or his or her address or any school as being that of a child involved in proceedings (Article 170 of the Children Order). Documents filed in court are confidential and may only be disclosed without leave of the court to a party, the legal representative of a party, the guardian ad litem, the Legal Services Commission or a welfare officer (Family Proceedings Rule 4.24). A child may not be medically or psychiatrically examined or otherwise assessed without leave of the court. Any evidence obtained as a result of an unauthorised examination or assessment is not admissible without leave of the court (Rule 4.19). In public law proceedings, no one can decline to give evidence or to answer a question put to him or her in the course of his or her evidence on the ground of self-incrimination. No statement or admission made in the

---

2   Having regard to the wishes and feelings of a child does not necessarily mean agreeing with or giving effect to them.

course of such proceedings is admissible in evidence against the person making it or his or her spouse in proceedings for an offence other than perjury (Article 171 of the Children Order).

Allocation

There are three levels of court in which proceedings may be heard:

- the Family Proceedings Court;
- the Family Care Centre; and
- the Family Division of the High Court.

Nearly all proceedings commence in the Family Proceedings Court. Most are heard there but some are transferred up to the Family Care Centre and fewer still from the Family Care Centre to the High Court. The structure for the transfer of proceedings is set out in the Children (Allocation of Proceedings) Order (Northern Ireland) 1996. Guidance on the proper level of court can be found in the Appendix to the *Guide to Case Management in Public Law Proceedings*. The guidance in the Appendix is common to both public and private law proceedings.

5

Hearing the voice of the child

Private law proceedings

Ordinarily, a child is not a party to private law proceedings, which are largely (although not necessarily) disputes between parents as to what is best for the child. There are good reasons why a child should not be put in a position in which he or she may feel that a choice has to be made between parents. In most cases, the court will try to find out what a child thinks by requesting a report under Article 4 of the Children Order from a "suitably qualified person", usually a social worker employed by a Trust. This can take between six and eight weeks and this period is allowed for in the *Guide to Private Law Proceedings*. The social worker will speak to the parents and may offer mediation.

Sometimes a child is old enough and mature enough to want to engage in proceedings. In order to do so in private law proceedings, the child will need the leave of the court. Courts are acute to detect circumstances in which a child is being influenced by a parent, usually the residential parent, to express a view that coincides with the view of that parent. Such influence is a form of child abuse and is always counter-productive. While there is an increasing tendency to allow "competent" children to be parties to proceedings,[1] the court will always want to know what the child's participation will add to the proceedings. Being a party to proceedings imposes duties as well as conferring rights and the court will want to be satisfied that a proposed child party is aware of and able to shoulder the duties as well as the rights of being a party, for example, in relation to confidentiality and disclosure of documents.

1   See *Mabon v Mabon* [2005] EWCA Civ 634, [2005] 2 FLR 1011.

Competence – the ability to decide an issue for oneself – depends on the issue to be decided and the maturity and understanding of the child involved,[2] It also involves a degree of foresight and an understanding of how others are likely to react. The youngest person known to have been found to be competent and to have participated in proceedings in the High Court in Northern Ireland was a girl aged 12, described by the judge as quite exceptional.

Ordinarily, a minor has to be represented by a next friend in order to bring proceedings, or a guardian ad litem in order to defend proceedings. Both the next friend or the guardian ad litem must be adults who have no interest in the outcome of the proceedings. If there is no such person, then the Official Solicitor may consent to act as next friend or guardian ad litem for the child. In private law proceedings, a child may act without a next friend or guardian ad litem where he or she obtains leave to do so from the court or where a solicitor considers that the child has sufficient understanding to give him or her instructions in relation to the proceedings and has agreed to act (see Rules 6.2 and 6.3 of the Family Proceedings Rules (NI) 1996).

The High Court or the Family Care Centre may request the Official Solicitor to either report to the court on the best interests of children in private law proceedings, and/or represent them as guardian ad litem in such proceedings.

It is unusual for a judge to interview children in private law proceedings. However, if a child asks to see the judge, he/she will usually not be refused an interview. If the judge does interview the child, an independent person will accompany the child and take a note of what is said. There ought to be no secrets between the judge and the child and the notes taken by the independent person will ordinarily be made available to the parties. The child will be made aware of this before the interview takes place.

2   The classic exposition of competence remains the speech of Lord Scarman in *Gillick v West Norfolk & Wisbech AHA* [1986] 1 FLR 224, but see also *Re H A (a Minor) (Care Proceedings: Child's Wishes)* [1993] 1 FLR 440, *Re S (a Minor) (Independent Representation)* [1993] 2 FLR 347, and *Re M (Minors) (Care Proceedings: Child's Wishes)* [1994] 1 FLR 748, all of which now have to be read subject to *Mabon v Mabon*.

Public law proceedings

The child is always a party to public law proceedings. Almost invariably, the child will be represented by a guardian ad litem employed by the **Northern Ireland Guardian ad Litem Agency (NIGALA)**, which is a public body independent of the Health and Social Care Trusts. A NIGALA guardian is to be distinguished from a guardian ad litem in private law proceedings and a testamentary guardian appointed by will or deed. A NIGALA guardian will come from a social work or probation service background and will be appointed solely for the purposes of the specified proceedings before the court either under Part V of the Children Order, or under the Adoption Order, or both. The guardian's powers and duties are limited by the relevant statute and the proceedings in respect of which the guardian is appointed. If the guardian is of the opinion that the interests of the child require that some other form of proceedings, such as a judicial review, ought to be taken in the interests of the child, then the guardian or the child's solicitor should report this to the Official Solicitor, who will decide whether to initiate proceedings.

The guardian's duties are to safeguard the interests of the child in the manner prescribed by the rules (Article 60(2) of the Children Order). In order to do so, the guardian has the right to examine and take copies of all records of or held by an authority (a Trust) or an authorised person (the NSPCC or some other person authorised by the Department to bring public law proceedings), which were compiled in connection with the making, or proposed making, by any person of any application under the Children Order with respect to the child concerned, and any records of or held by an authority or authorised person that relate to the child concerned (Article 61 of the Children Order), and such records are admissible in evidence. The definition of records that relate to the child concerned is wide enough to include records relating to a sibling or other relative.

The Rules referred to in Article 60(2) are in Part IV of the Family Proceedings Rules, particularly Rule 4.12. The guardian is to give advice to the child in accordance with the child's level of understanding and to instruct a solicitor to act in the proceedings on the child's behalf. The guardian is to advise the court as to:

a) whether the child is of sufficient understanding for any purpose, including submission to a medical, psychiatric or other examination or assessment that the court has power to order;

b) the wishes of the child in respect of any relevant matter, including attendance at court;

c) the appropriate forum for the proceedings;

d) the appropriate timing of the proceedings or any part of them;

e) the options available in respect of the child and the suitability of each such option, including what order should be made in determining the application;

f) any other matter in respect of which the court seeks the guardian's advice or concerning which the guardian considers that the court should be informed.

The guardian has the power to notify any person whose participation in the proceedings as a party is, in the guardian's opinion, likely to safeguard the interests of the child, of the proceedings and that person's ability to apply to be joined as a party. The guardian has to report to the court as directed by the court and, in any event, not less than seven days before trial. The guardian can make such inquiries as appear to be necessary for the performance of his or her duties and can obtain professional assistance. There is no geographical limit to the guardian's inquiries.[3] After the case is over, the guardian is to explain to the child what has happened, assuming the child to have sufficient understanding, and instruct the child's solicitor as to the merits of an appeal.

If it appears that an apparently competent child wishes to instruct his or her solicitor directly, then the guardian should cease instructing the solicitor. If appropriate, the guardian can seek leave to engage independent legal representation. If the child so wishes, the solicitor instructed by the guardian should offer to continue to represent the child unless the solicitor

---

3   *Re N and L (Care Order: Investigations by Guardian ad Litem outside Northern Ireland)* (2003) (GILC3855).

also represents other children in the proceedings. In the latter event, representation should be offered through another solicitor on the NIGALA panel.

It has not been known for a child to seek separate representation in adoption proceedings.

6

Parental responsibility

What is parental responsibility?

Parental responsibility is the responsibility that each parent has to the child. By Article 6(1) of the Children Order, it means 'all the rights, duties, powers, responsibilities and authority which by law a parent of a child has in relation to the child and his property'. It includes the power to consent to medical treatment where the child is not of sufficient age and understanding to do so, and the power to consent to marriage.

Who has parental responsibility?

At birth, the mother always has parental responsibility for the child. The father, if married to the mother at the time of birth, shares parental responsibility with her from the time of birth. If the parents are unmarried at the time of birth but subsequently marry, then the father acquires parental responsibility from the date of marriage. If the father is not married to the mother, then he can acquire parental responsibility:

a) if his name appears as the child's father on the child's birth certificate, if registered after 15 April 2002;

b) if he enters into a parental responsibility agreement with the mother and registers it with the court; or

c) if the court, on his application, orders that he should have parental responsibility for the child.

In the last of these, the court will expect the applicant to have demonstrated some degree of commitment to the child before making an order.

The court can also order that a step-parent should have parental responsibility for the child.

If a residence order is made in favour of someone who does not have parental responsibility for a child, then such a person acquires parental responsibility by virtue of the residence order while it remains in place.

Where all those with parental responsibility have died or no longer have parental responsibility for the child, the High Court, on the application of any person, may order that person to be the child's guardian. Such an order can also be made in family proceedings even if no person has applied for such an order.

A parent with parental responsibility can appoint another person to be the child's guardian after the first person's death. Such an appointment has to be made by will or deed or a written and dated instrument by the person making the appointment or at his direction, in his presence and in the presence of two witnesses, each of whom attests the signature. Such an appointment can be revoked before death by one of the means by which it can be made or by the making of a subsequent appointment. Such an appointment does not take effect if someone still living has parental responsibility for the child.

Where parental responsibility is shared, then those who have parental responsibility have to act together in taking any important decisions for the child. If they cannot agree, then the court will decide what to do in the best interests of the child if an application is made for a specific issues order.

A Trust acquires parental responsibility on the making of a care order (including an interim care order). It shares that parental responsibility with the parent(s) who have parental responsibility, but has the power to determine the extent to which a parent or guardian of the child may meet his or her parental responsibility. However, it cannot cause the child to be brought up in any religious persuasion other than that in which he or she would have been brought up if the order had not been made, cannot consent to the making of a freeing or adoption order in respect of the child, and cannot appoint a guardian for the child. When a care order is in force, no person can cause the child to be known by any other name or remove him or her from the UK without the consent in writing of every person who has parental responsibility or the leave of the court, provided that a Trust can consent to the removal of a child for a temporary period of not more than one month (usually in the case of a child going on holiday with foster carers) or if arrangements have been made under Article 33 of the Children Order with the approval of the court.

Parental responsibility vests in the applicant on the making of an emergency protection order.

How is parental responsibility lost?

Parental responsibility is only lost:

a) on the child attaining the age of 18;

b) on the making of a freeing order, in which event parental responsibility vests in the adoption agency in whose favour the freeing order is made;

c) on the making of an adoption order, in which event parental responsibility vests in the person(s) in whose favour the adoption order is made; and

d) in the case of an unmarried father or a step-parent, by order of the court to that effect.

The Surrogacy Arrangements Act 1985 and the Human Fertilisation and Embryology Acts apply to Northern Ireland in the same way as they do to the rest of the UK.

7

The child at home

There is no statutory regulation of children at home.

- The extent to which a child requires supervision will vary in the light of the age of the child and the child's own characteristics.

- The parent is entitled to make suitable arrangements for supervision of the child but may incur liabilities if the child is not supervised by proper persons.

- The parent is expected to provide the child with the care which it would be reasonable to expect a parent to give him or her. If a failure to provide care of that standard gives rise to the child sustaining significant harm or being likely to sustain significant harm, the relevant Trust may intervene.

Child care and day care

Child care and day care for young children are regulated by Part XI of the Children Order and persons who provide such care for one or more children for reward for more than two hours per day have to be registered with the relevant Trust. It is an offence to provide such facilities without being registered. Registration is not required if the person providing care is a relative of the child, has parental responsibility for the child or is a foster carer, nor is it required of a nanny looking after children mainly in the home of an employer.

Private foster care

Private foster care arises where a child is looked after or is intended to be looked after for a period of 28 days or more by someone who is not a parent of the child or a person who has parental responsibility for him or her or who is a relative of the child. Private foster care does not arise where a child is attending a boarding school (unless he or she stays there for a period of more than two weeks during school holidays) or is in hospital.[1] The Children (Private Arrangements for Fostering) Regulations 1996 require prospective foster carers to notify the relevant Trust of their intention to foster not less than six nor more than 13 weeks before receipt of the child into foster care. The Trust has a duty to ensure the welfare of privately fostered children and it discharges this duty by periodic visits to such children.

1   For the full list of exceptions, see Article 107 of the Children Order.

8

General duties of Health and Social Care Trusts

Children in need

A child is taken as being in need if he or she is unlikely to achieve or maintain, or have the opportunity of achieving or maintaining, a reasonable standard of health or development without the provision to him or her of services by a Trust, or his or her health or development is likely to be significantly impaired, or further impaired without the provisions of such services, or he or she is disabled (Article 17 of the Children Order). Trusts are under a general duty to safeguard and promote the welfare of children in need in their areas and to promote the upbringing of such children by their families by providing a range of personal social services.

The duties of Trusts to children in need

- Whether or not a child is in need, Trusts are required to provide such day care as is appropriate for children under five in their areas who are not attending school.

- Trusts are required to provide for children in need such care or supervised activities as are appropriate outside school hours and during school holidays (Article 19 of the Children Order).

- Specific duties are imposed in respect of children who are disabled and children who are themselves carers.

- Trusts are obliged to provide accommodation for any child in need in respect of whom there is no person with parental responsibility, or who is lost or abandoned or if the person who has been caring for him or her is prevented from providing suitable accommodation or care.

- Before providing accommodation under this Article, an authority shall, as far as is reasonably practical, ascertain the child's wishes regarding the provision of accommodation and shall give due consideration, having regard to his age and understanding, to the wishes of the child.[1] Regional good practice guidance has been issued jointly by the Northern Ireland Housing Executive and the Health and Social Care Board which clearly sets out the duty to meet the accommodation and support needs of 16–21-year-olds under Article 21 of the Children Order and the agreed procedures to be followed by the NIHE and the Trusts to discharge their duties effectively under this provision of the Order.

- Persons with parental responsibility can agree to a child being accommodated by an authority ("voluntary accommodation"), but that agreement can be revoked at will and, on such revocation, the child must be returned unless there is a care order or interim care order in force.

---

1   Article 21(6) of the Children Order.

9

Private law orders

Orders available in private law proceedings

The orders available in private law proceedings are set out below.

Residence orders

This is an order settling the arrangements to be made as to the person with whom the child is to live. Such an order simply settles the practical arrangements regarding with whom a child is to live. It does not alter the child's legal relationship with his or her parents nor does it confer any particular status on the parent with whom the child is to live for the time being over the other parent. Where a child spends a significant period of time with both parents, this may be recognised by a joint residence order that specifies how much time the child is to spend with each parent. The granting of a joint residence order does not confer any particular status on one parent over the other.

Contact orders

This is an order requiring the person with whom a child lives, or is to live, to allow the child to visit or stay with the person named in the order or for that person or the child otherwise to have contact with each other. A contact order may be made in respect of a child who is voluntarily accommodated by a Trust. In general, the courts try to encourage and facilitate contact between a child and both parents, provided that that contact is beneficial and safe for the child. It should be noted that contact is always for the benefit of the child and not the parent.

Prohibited steps orders

This is an order which prevents a person who has parental responsibility for the child taking any step specified in the order which that person would otherwise have been entitled to take in the exercise of parental responsibility. It is usually employed where persons sharing parental responsibility cannot agree on what is to be done and one parent desires to retain the status quo until the issue can be resolved.

Specific issue orders

This is an order giving directions for the purpose of determining a specific question that has arisen, or that may arise, in connection with any aspect of parental responsibility.

These are known as **Article 8 orders**.

In substance, a parent or guardian of a child and any person in whose favour a residence order is in force can apply for any Article 8 order. Any person (other than a Trust foster carer) with whom a child has lived for three years can apply for a residence order or a contact order. A Trust foster carer can apply for an Article 8 order if he or she has the consent of the Trust, or is a relative of the child, or if the child has lived with him or her for a period of three years in the last five years.

Anyone else has to apply to the court for leave to seek an Article 8 order. On such an application, the court has to pay particular regard to:

● the nature of the application;

● the applicant's connection with the child; and

● any risk there might be of the proposed application disrupting the child's life to such an extent that he or she would be harmed by it.

● Where the child is being looked after by a Trust, the court also has to pay regard to the plans of the Trust for the child and the wishes and feelings of the child's parents (Article 10(9) of the Children Order).

An Article 8 order can contain conditions and may be expressed to have effect for a specified period.

The court has power to make an order for financial relief with respect to children (Article 15 and Schedule 1 to the Children Order).

The court may also make a **family assistance order**, which is an order requiring a Trust to make a suitably qualified person available to advise, assist and (where appropriate) befriend the parents or guardian of the child, any person with whom the child is living or in whose favour a contact order is in force, or the child himself or herself. The order only has effect for six months or such shorter period as may be specified in the order (Article 16 of the Children Order).

An Article 8 order ordinarily comes to an end when the child attains the age of 16, but it can be extended in exceptional circumstances until the child attains 18 (Article 9(6) of the Children Order).

Private law proceedings are governed by the Family Proceedings Rules and the *Guide to Case Management in Private Law Proceedings*. The parties are expected to have corresponded prior to the issue of proceedings with a view to resolving the issues between them or, at least, limiting the issues. They are expected to have considered whether some form of alternative dispute resolution (ADR), such as conciliation, might help them. When proceedings are issued, the court will actively case manage things with a view to obtaining the best information as early as possible in order to decide the issues between the parties. The court will encourage, in appropriate cases, the use of ADR and reports or issues arising out of ADR are reviewed at each stage of the process to consider whether the case can be resolved without the need for a court order. Such measures and procedures serve to promote early agreement between parties and discourage protraction of court proceedings but it is recognised that in some cases, particularly those involving violence or mental abuse or where previous agreements or court orders have failed, that ADR may be inappropriate or may only serve to delay resolution of a dispute. *The Guide to Case Management in Private Law Proceedings* outlines the role of ADR in private family proceedings in some detail.[1] Some forms of ADR, if directed by the court, may attract public funding. Those providing ADR are expected to report to the court as directed as to the areas of dispute and agreement between the parties and the parties, by engaging in ADR directed by the court, are taken to have waived any privilege that they might otherwise have had. Ultimately, whatever agreement may be reached by the parties, the court will decide what is best for the child.

If in any family proceedings it appears to the court that a public law remedy may be appropriate, the court may direct a Trust to carry out an investigation of the child's circumstances (Article 56 of the Children Order). On such an investigation, that Trust has to consider whether to apply for a public law order or to provide any service to the child and his or her family, or take any other action with respect to the child. The Trust is expected to report back to the court within eight weeks or such other time as the court may direct.

1   See paragraphs 10.1 -10.5, page 16, *Guide to Case Management in Private Law Proceedings*.

10

Public law orders

Emergency protection orders

The court can make an emergency protection order if satisfied that there is reasonable ground to believe that the child is likely to suffer significant harm if he or she is not removed to accommodation provided by the Trust, or that the Trust is making inquiries about the child and that access to the child is being unreasonably refused and that the Trust has reason to believe that access to the child is required as a matter of urgency. An emergency protection order authorises the removal of the child into Trust accommodation and the child being kept there and it gives the Trust parental responsibility for the child.

Applications for emergency protection orders are usually made with only the Trust being present and the court is obliged to keep a careful note of the evidence given and the grounds advanced for the making of the order. The order can include a requirement excluding a person from a dwelling-house in which the child lives. The order can only have effect for eight days, after which the Trust, if it so wishes, must bring before the court an application for a care order. The parent(s) can apply to discharge an emergency protection order at any time.[1] Exceptionally, a constable, who suspects that a child would otherwise be likely to suffer significant harm, may remove a child to suitable accommodation for a period not exceeding 72 hours but he or she must, as soon as reasonably practicable, inform the child's parents of what has been done and why, and of any further steps that may be taken (Article 65 of the Children Order).

1   A provision preventing such an application for 72 hours was held to be incompatible with the ECHR and was removed.

Threshold

In order to obtain a public law order under the Children Order, the Trust must prove, on the balance of probabilities, that the child is suffering or is likely to suffer significant harm either due to the care given to the child or likely to be given to him or her if an order were not made, not being what it would be reasonable to expect a parent to give to him or her, or to the child's being beyond parental control (Article 50(2) of the Children Order). The court must make findings either upon hearing evidence or by concessions from the parents. The court is not bound to accept concessions and has to be satisfied, in the interests of the child, that concessions meet the substance of the case. The relevant date for satisfying the threshold conditions is either the date of commencement of the proceedings or, where protective measures (including voluntary accommodation) have been in place, the date upon which those measures were put into effect.[2] If a Trust is uncertain as to whether an application for a care order or a supervision order is appropriate and it wishes to have an assessment of a child's health or development in order to determine whether threshold criteria have been attained, it may apply for a child assessment order to enable such an assessment to take place (Article 62 of the Children Order).

The orders

The primary public law orders are:

- **care orders**
- **supervision orders**

Care orders

A **care order** is an order placing the child in the care of the Trust. The Trust shares parental responsibility with the parents but can determine the extent to which a parent may meet his or her parental responsibility. There is no time limit to a care order, other than the child attaining the age of majority.

---

2   *Homefirst CHSST v SA* [2001] NIJB 218.

Supervision orders

A **supervision order** is an order requiring a specified person (the supervisor) to advise, assist and befriend the supervised child. The supervisor can require the child to live at a specified place, to present himself to a person specified, and to participate in activities specified. A person who has parental responsibility or with whom the child is living may be required to take all reasonable steps to ensure that the child complies with the order. The child may also be required to submit to a medical or psychiatric assessment. A supervision order lasts for a year but can be extended to a maximum period of three years from the date upon which it was made (see Schedule 3 to the Children Order), but not beyond the child attaining the age of 18.

The court has power to make an **interim care order** or an **interim supervision order** where it is satisfied that there are reasonable grounds for believing that threshold criteria are met (Article 57 of the Children Order). Interim orders have the same effect as full orders but only last, in the first instance, for eight weeks and thereafter can only be renewed for a period of four weeks. It is usual for a succession of interim orders to be made until the case is disposed of by the court. A court making an interim order can also give directions as to the medical or psychiatric assessment of the child. An exclusion requirement can be attached to an interim care order (Article 57A of the Children Order). A Practice Note of 20 February 2003 (Long and Loughron, 2004) deals with the renewal of interim care orders without the necessity of the presence of the parties where there has been no material change of circumstances.

The care plan

In Northern Ireland, the care plan is not a creature of statute. Nevertheless, the court will not make a final order unless it is satisfied with the Trust's care plan for the child (except insofar as contact is concerned). A care plan is a plan 'which is sufficiently firm and particularised for all concerned to have a reasonably clear picture of the likely way ahead for the child in the foreseeable future'.[3] There is usually a degree of uncertainty. It is a matter

3   See *Re S, Re W (Minors)* [2002] UKHL 10, para.99.

for the court whether such uncertainties as exist can or ought to be resolved before a final order is made. The reality is that care planning takes up much of the time of the court. If the court does not agree with the provisions of the care plan in relation to contact, it can make its own order as to contact under Article 53 of the Children Order.[4]

Discharge

The Trust, a parent or other person having parental responsibility for the child can apply for the discharge of a care order or a supervision order, but in order to obtain a discharge it is necessary to show a significant change in circumstances. The making of a residence order discharges a prior care or supervision order. A care order discharges any prior Article 8 order.

Conduct of public law proceedings

Public law proceedings are conducted in accordance with the Family Proceedings Rules and the *Guide to Case Management in Public Law Proceedings*. Practice Directions deal with the filing of bundles and time estimates. The Guide does not apply to emergency applications.

In all other public law proceedings, the Trust is expected to have written to the parents before issuing proceedings, setting out the Trust's concerns and inviting them to a meeting to resolve issues without the need for proceedings. Parents may be legally represented at such a meeting and public funding may be available in respect of such representation.

The Trust's application should set out the facts upon which the Trust intends to rely in proving threshold. There should be full disclosure of documents at an early stage and the parents will be expected to reply to the Trust allegations. All public law cases will be actively case-managed by the court and this may include separate hearings to resolve specific issues where that is in the best interests of the child. It is not unusual for threshold issues to be decided at an early stage prior to consideration of care planning.

4   *Re SB (a Child)* [2002] NIJB 137.

11

The child in care

Objectives

- The courts will try to reunite a child with his or her parents as soon as possible, if that can be achieved safely and is in the child's best interests.

- If a return home cannot be achieved, a placement will be sought within the child's extended family.

- If neither of these outcomes can be achieved, attention will be given to finding the child a new family, possibly through foster care, but more usually through adoption.

Planning will be concurrent and not consecutive so as to avoid delay. While reunification is the initial object, children cannot be expected to wait indefinitely while parents make required changes. Time, therefore, inevitably begins to run against the parents once a child is taken into care. They usually have but one opportunity to make changes, after which alternative placements will become the priority.

Looked after children

A **looked after child** is a child who is in the care of a Trust or who is provided with accommodation by a Trust for a continuous period of more than 24 hours.

In respect of all looked after children, the Trust is under a duty to safeguard and promote his or her welfare and make use of such services available for children cared for by their own parents as appears reasonable. The Trust is expected to discover and take into account the wishes and feelings of the child, his or her parents, anyone else who has parental responsibility, and any other person whom the Trust considers relevant. The Trust has to provide the child with accommodation and to maintain him or her. In general, the Trust is to maintain and promote contact between the child and his or her wider family.

Children living outside Northern Ireland

Under Article 33 of the Children Order, the Trust can only arrange for or assist the child living outside Northern Ireland with the approval of the court. The court has to be satisfied:

- that living outside Northern Ireland would be in the child's best interests;

- that suitable arrangements have been made or will be made for the child's reception and welfare in the country in which he or she will live;

- that the child consents to living in that country; and

- that every person who has parental responsibility has consented. Consent of a person with parental responsibility can be dispensed with if that person cannot be found, is incapable of consenting or is withholding consent unreasonably.

Reviews

The principal decision-making body in relation to a looked after child is the Looked After Child (LAC) Review. The LAC Review is a multi-disciplinary meeting including all those who are likely to be involved in care planning for the child. It includes the parents and the child's guardian ad litem where one has been appointed.

The first LAC Review is to take place within two weeks of the child becoming looked after, the second three months after the first, and any subsequent reviews at six-monthly intervals. These are maximum times and LAC Reviews may be convened more frequently. The matters to be considered at the LAC Review are stipulated by Regulations (Review of Children's Cases Regulations (Northern Ireland) 1996).

Placements

When a child is taken into care, the Trust is expected to plan not just the immediate placement but also the long-term arrangements for the placement and for promoting the welfare of the child. The manner in which this is to be done and the matters to be taken into account are specified by Regulations (Arrangements for Placement of Children (General) Regulations (Northern Ireland) 1996).

Placement will usually be with a foster carer from a Trust or from an independent fostering provider, with a kinship carer, or, less usually, in a children's home provided by the Trust. The Trust can access specialist foster carers, who may be contracted out to a different agency or specialist care homes that may best be placed to meet the needs of the child. The Foster Placement (Children) Regulations (Northern Ireland) 1996 govern the approval of foster carers, who may be generally approved or specifically approved for an individual child, the considerations to be taken into account in affecting placements, agreements to be made between the Trust and the specific foster carer(s) and the periodic (at least monthly) visits to the child on behalf of the Trust. There are also detailed Regulations that govern the placement of a child in care back with his parent(s) (the Placement of Children with Parents etc. Regulations (Northern Ireland) 1996).

Contact with a child in care

Under Article 53 of the Children Order, the Trust is to allow reasonable contact between a child in care and his or her parents. The Trust, the child or the parents may apply to the court for an order (a **care contact order**) specifying the contact which is to be allowed. This can include a provision that no contact be permitted between the child and a parent. A Trust can decide in a case of urgency to refuse contact for a period of no more than seven days – if it wishes to continue to refuse contact thereafter, it must bring the matter to court. The reality is that the Trust will always seek court approval for any reduction in contact even if the parents agree. The Contact with Children Regulations (Northern Ireland) 1996 require the Trust to notify certain persons, including the child and the parents, of any intention to refuse, vary or suspend contact arrangements.

Complaints

The Representations Procedure (Children) Regulations (Northern Ireland) 1996 provide for a process for dealing with complaints about the discharge of a Trust's duties under Part IV of the Children Order. In substance, the Trust is to appoint an independent person to take part in the Trust's considerations of the complaint. If the complainant is dissatisfied with the Trust's response to his or her complaint, he or she can ask for the matter to be referred to a panel that should include at least one independent person and which should meet within 28 days of the matter being referred. The panel makes a recommendation to the Trust, which will then decide what action to take. The decision of the Trust may be susceptible to judicial review.

Leaving care

Articles 34A–36 of the Children Order contain provisions requiring the Trust to plan for the future of any child leaving care including the provision of services both before and after leaving care. These supplementary provisions were inserted in Part IV of the Children Order by the Children (Leaving Care) Act (NI) 2002 and the Children (Leaving Care) Regulations (NI) 2005 and came into operation on 1 September 2005. The aim of these provisions was to improve the assessment, preparation and planning processes for young people leaving care and also to provide better personal and financial supports for those who have left care. The Children (Leaving Care) Regulations (NI) 2005 builds on the Act and provides more detail on the Trust's duties, in particular, the assessment of young people's needs, preparation of the Pathway Plan and the functions of a personal adviser. There are three categories of child who are entitled to varying levels of aftercare services from the Trusts, namely the eligible child, the relevant child and the former relevant child. The eligible child is a young person aged 16 or 17 who is still looked after and has been looked after for a period of at least 13 weeks since the age of 14. The relevant child is a young person aged 16 or 17 who has ceased to be looked after but was looked after for at least 13 weeks since reaching the age of 14. The former relevant child is an adult aged 18–21 who has left care and before leaving care was either an eligible child or a relevant child or both. Eligible children are entitled to a personal adviser, a needs assessment and a Pathway Plan, in addition to all the entitlements of the looked after system, as they are still looked after children. Relevant children are entitled to a personal adviser, a needs assessment, a Pathway Plan, accommodation and financial assistance to meet the young person's needs in relation to education, training, or employment as provided for in the Pathway Plan, and the Trust must keep in touch with the young person. Former relevant children are entitled to have their personal adviser and their Pathway Plan continue until they are 21. They are also entitled to continuing advice and assistance, including assistance with employment, education and training, and also accommodation during vacations from higher education if needed.

Secure accommodation

A **secure accommodation order** is an order under Article 44 of the Children Order authorising a Trust to place a child who is being looked after by it in secure accommodation, which means accommodation provided for the purpose of restricting liberty. A Trust cannot place a child in secure accommodation without an order of the court beyond an aggregate period of 72 hours in any period of 28 days. The grounds for placing a child in secure accommodation are that he or she has a history of absconding and is likely to abscond from any other description of accommodation and, if he or she absconds, he or she is likely to suffer significant harm, or that if he or she is kept in any other description of accommodation, he or she is likely to injure himself or herself or other persons. The maximum period for which a court may authorise a child to be kept in secure accommodation is three months, but it may authorise a child to be kept in secure accommodation for a further period not exceeding six months at any one time.

The placing of a child in secure accommodation is a severe restriction on liberty so the provisions of the Human Rights Act are always engaged. The child's parents or other persons having parental responsibility have to be notified of the application and the child has to be legally represented unless having been informed of his or her entitlement to legal aid, and having had an opportunity to do so, he or she has failed to apply. The child must be physically present in court other than in exceptional circumstances.[1] The welfare checklist does not apply.[2]

Relocation and abduction

Internal relocation

There is no statutory prohibition on relocation of children within the UK, but it can be restrained by use of a **prohibited steps order**. Alternatively, if a **contact order** is in place, it may be necessary to apply to vary such an order. In either eventuality, the court will be concerned with the best interests of each child involved.

External relocation

Article 13 of the Children Order prohibits, where a **residence order** is in force with respect to a child, the removal of that child from the UK for a period of more than one month without the written consent of every person who has parental responsibility for that child or the leave of the court. Even where no residence order is in place, the consent of every person having parental responsibility would be necessary for such a major event in the child's life and a failure to obtain such consent would be likely to result in an enforced return under the provisions of the 1980 Hague Convention (assuming that the relocation was to a signatory of that Convention). The welfare checklist does not apply to an application under Article 13 but the best interests of the child are paramount.

The Court of Appeal in Northern Ireland has affirmed that the courts in

1   *North & West Belfast H&SST v DH* [2001] NI 351.
2   *Re AK* [2000] 205.

Northern Ireland are not bound by the decision of the Court of Appeal in England in *Payne v Payne*[3] while according decisions of that court due respect as persuasive authority, particularly when considering the same or a similar legislative provision. It held that the welfare of the child is the paramount consideration in relocation cases and that, as a matter of good practice, the starting point ought to be a consideration of the welfare checklist even when it may not strictly apply. While the factors mentioned in *Payne v Payne* may be relevant in some cases, there is a risk that guidance 'may give rise to separate disputes and may distract the judge from the statutory test as a result of a mechanistic application of the guidance'. There is no need for further guidance in Northern Ireland.[4]

Consequently, each case will depend on its own facts although first instance decisions indicate that where there is beneficial and extensive contact between the child and an absent parent which would be restricted by a relocation, the loss of such contact is likely to carry significant weight.[5]

Abduction

The UK is a signatory to the 1980 Hague Convention, the Convention on the Civil Aspects of International Child Abduction, which is incorporated into domestic law by the Child Abduction and Custody Act 1985. The object of the Convention is to ensure the speedy return of any child under 16 brought from another signatory state into the UK, in which the child was habitually resident, in breach of the rights of custody attributed to a person, institution or other body. It also applies where a child is unlawfully retained in the UK. The Convention is enforced by the Central Authority of the state in which the child is found.

The court must order the return of a child to the original state of habitual residence if the application is made within one year of the removal or retention. If the application is made outside that period, the court must

---

3   [2001] EWCA Civ 166.
4   *SH v RD* [2013] NICA 44 and *Re L* [2013] NICA 46.
5   See *SL v RG* [2012] NIFam 1 and *SH v RD & RH* [2012[NIFam2.

still order the return unless it appears that the child is settled in the new environment at the date of issue of the proceedings. Article 13 of the Convention provides defences that either the custody rights were not being exercised, or the person able to exercise them consented to or subsequently acquiesced in the removal or retention, or there is a grave risk that a return would expose the child to physical or psychological harm or otherwise place the child in an intolerable situation. These defences are difficult to establish. The Brussels IIb Regulations amend the application of the Convention in a number of respects, chiefly so as to provide that the child is provided with an opportunity to be heard, to provide that the court is to act expeditiously so as to give judgment within six weeks after the issue of proceedings (other than in exceptional circumstances), and to provide that a return cannot be refused on the basis of grave risk of harm or an intolerable situation if adequate arrangements have been made to secure the child after the return (Article 11 of the Brussels IIb Regulations). Suggestions from the European Court of Human Rights that the domestic court is to carry out a careful assessment of the child's home conditions before ordering a return seem inconsistent with the six-week time limit and have been doubted.

The court is likely to apply the terms of the Convention where return is sought to a non-Convention country on the basis that it is usually in the best interests of a child to have his or her future determined in the courts of the country in which he or she is habitually resident.

Wardship

The use of the inherent jurisdiction of the High Court to make a child a ward of court is now significantly restricted. It cannot be used to place a child in care or under supervision by a Trust, or to require a child to be accommodated by a Trust, or to make a child a ward of court who is subject to a care order, or to confer power on a trust to determine any question in relation to the exercise of parental responsibility for a child (Article 173 of the Children Order). A Trust can no longer apply for a wardship order without leave of the court and that leave will only be granted if the result that the Trust seeks to achieve cannot be attained in any other way, and there is reasonable cause to believe that if the inherent jurisdiction is not exercised the child is likely to suffer significant harm.

Nevertheless, the inherent jurisdiction still has a significant role to play, particularly in emergency situations, because on making the application the child immediately becomes a ward of court (Section 26(2) of the Judicature (Northern Ireland) Act 1978). This is particularly material if it is suspected that an attempt is about to be or is being made to remove a child from the jurisdiction unlawfully, as it enables a port alert to be initiated, which will result in the child being detained pending the direction of the court. It is also of considerable assistance where a child has been abducted to or unlawfully retained in a country that is not a signatory to the 1980 Hague Convention, for example, India, where it may carry weight with the domestic courts. It also enables the court to access consular services for the child abroad. While the court has power under Section 37 of the Family Law Act 1986 to require surrender of a UK passport, it can only require the surrender of a foreign passport in wardship.

Wardship also has a significant role in relation to the determination of questions relating to the provision of medical treatment, where that treatment is refused by an apparently competent child or a child's parent(s) against medical advice.

12

Adoption

The system of adoption currently in force in Northern Ireland is similar to that which applied in England and Wales before January 2006. It is understood that consideration is being given to changing to a system similar to that which applies in England and Wales as at the time of writing (summer 2013).

The principles

In deciding upon any course of action in relation to the adoption of a child, the court and any adoption agency shall regard the welfare of the child as the most important consideration and shall –

(a) have regard to all the circumstances, full consideration being given to:
(i) the need to be satisfied that adoption, or adoption by a particular person or persons will be in the best interests of the child; and
(ii) the need to safeguard and promote the welfare of the child throughout his childhood; and
(iii) the importance of providing the child with a stable and harmonious home; and

(b) so far as practicable, first ascertain the wishes and feelings of the child regarding the decision and give due consideration to them having regard to his age and understanding.

(Article 9 of the Adoption (Northern Ireland) Order 1987)

It is unlawful for anyone other than a registered adoption agency to make arrangements for the adoption of a child unless he or she is a parent of the child and the proposed adopter, or one of the proposed adopters is a relative of the child, or he or she is acting in pursuance of an order of the High Court. The adoption agencies in Northern Ireland are the Health and Social Care Trusts and the registered adoption agencies.

Subject to certain exceptions relating to registered adoption agencies or the obtaining of leave of the court, it is an offence to make any payment or reward whatever in connection with the adoption of any child. It is an offence to publish any advertisement indicating that a parent wants to cause a child to be adopted or that a person wants to adopt a child or that a person, other than a registered adoption agency, is willing to make any arrangements for the adoption of a child.

Who can adopt?

- A married couple can adopt where both are over the age of 21.

- A married couple can adopt where one of them is the father or mother of the child and the other is 21.

- A single person over the age of 21 can adopt.

- It has been held that the provisions of the adoption order that prevent an unmarried couple (whether of both or the same sex) adopting are incompatible with the European Convent on Human Rights. Consequently, the provisions of Article 15 of the Adoption Order, which provide that a married person can only adopt as a single person unless his spouse cannot be found, or the spouses are separate and are living apart and the separation is likely to be permanent, or the spouse is incapable of applying for an adoption order by reason of physical or mental ill-health, may also be incompatible.

- An adoption order cannot be made on the sole application of the mother or father of a child unless the other natural parent is dead or cannot be found or there is no other natural parent by virtue of section 28 of the Human Fertilisation and Embryology Act 1990 or there is some other reason justifying the exclusion of the other natural parent (which reason must be recorded by the court).

- There is no legal upper age limit for adopting a child.

Who can be adopted?

- Any child under the age of 18 can be adopted.

- Where the adopter is a parent, step-parent or relative of the child, or the child has been placed by an adoption agency or in pursuance of an order of the High Court, the child must be at least 19 weeks old and have had his or her home with the adopter at all times during the preceding 13 weeks.

- In all other cases, the child must be at least 12 months old and have had his or her home with the adopter at all times during the preceding 12 months.

The effect of the adoption order

An adoption order gives parental responsibility for the child to the adopters and extinguishes the parental responsibility previously held by any other person. It discharges any previous order made under the Children Order. An adopted child is treated in law as if he or she were the child of the adopter(s) and as if he or she were not the child of any other person, except that it does not affect the prohibited degrees in respect of marriage and does not affect the descent of any peerage or dignity or title of honour or any property or interest vested in possession. Where the adopters are married, the adopted child is treated as a child of the marriage.

An adoption order may be made subject to conditions.

Parental agreement to an adoption order

An adoption order cannot be made unless the child has been freed for adoption or the court is satisfied that each parent or guardian of the child freely agrees, either generally or in respect of a specific adopter, and either unconditionally or subject only to a condition as to the religious persuasion in which the child is to be brought up, to the making of the order or the court finds that his or her agreement to the making of the order should be dispensed with. The grounds for dispensing with parental agreement are that the parent or guardian:

(a) *cannot be found or is incapable of giving agreement;*

(b) *is withholding his agreement unreasonably;*

(c) *has persistently failed without reasonable cause to discharge his parental responsibility for the child;*

(d) *has abandoned or neglected the child;*

(e) *has persistently ill-treated the child; or*

(f) *has seriously ill-treated the child provided that rehabilitation within his household is unlikely.*

(Article 16 of the Adoption Order)

Consent by a mother is ineffective if given less than six weeks after the child was born.

Freeing

Despite suggestions that more use might be made of direct applications by prospective adopters without the child being freed for adoption,[1] the vast majority of contested applications proceed by way of **freeing**.

The object of the freeing procedure is for adoption agencies to find out if a child would be available for adoption before prospective adopters were found and their hopes frustrated if the adoption court ruled that consent was not being unreasonably withheld.[2]

Parents can consent to freeing either unconditionally or subject only to a condition as to the religious persuasion in which the child is to be brought up. The grounds for dispensing with consent are the same as those specified

---

1 For example, by Baroness Hale in *Down Lisburn Trust v H & R* [2006] UKHL 36.
2 *In re KLA (an Infant)* [2000] NI 234 approved in *Down Lisburn Trust v H & R*.

above in relation to the making of an adoption order. In addition to proving one of those grounds in respect of each parent, the applicant has to prove:

a) that the child is in the care of the adoption agency (i.e. because a care order, including an interim care order, has been made placing the child in the care of a Trust);

b) that the child has already been placed for adoption or is likely to be so placed within one year of the making of the freeing order;

c) that in the case of an unmarried father without parental responsibility, either he has no intention of applying for a parental responsibility order or a residence order in respect of the child or that, if he did make such an application, it would be likely to be refused;

d) that the adoption agency in deciding to apply for the order has complied with the relevant provisions of the Adoption Agencies Regulations; and

e) that each parent who can be found has been given an opportunity of making a declaration that he or she prefers not to be involved in future questions regarding the adoption of the child.

The making of a freeing order extinguishes the parental responsibility of all persons who previously had parental responsibility and gives it solely to the adoption agency.

Witholding consent unreasonably

The interpretation of the phrase 'is withholding his consent unreasonably' has given rise to much controversy, which has now been settled by a definitive judgment of the House of Lords, *Down Lisburn H&SST v H & R* [2006] UKHL 36. The test is an objective one which assumes that the parent has a full perception of his or her own limitations, a proper understanding of the evidence and the altruism needed to appreciate, if it be the case, that the interests of the child would be best served by adoption. In *Re C (a Minor) (Adoption: Parental Agreement: Contact)* [1993] 2 FLR 260, Steyn and Hoffmann LJJ formulated the test in terms of the judge asking himself whether, having regard to the evidence and the current values of society, the advantages of adoption for the welfare of the child appear sufficiently strong to justify overriding the views and interests of the objecting parent or parents. The use of that test in *Down Lisburn H&SST v H & R* was approved by the House of Lords. The European Court of Human Rights has held that the process set out in the adoption order is compatible with the provisions of the European Convention on Human Rights.

Revocation

Where a birth parent has declined to make a declaration that he or she prefers not to be involved in future questions about the child, the adoption agency must report to him or her within 14 days of the expiration of one year from the making of the freeing order whether an adoption order has been made and, if not, whether the child has his or her home with a person with whom he or she has been placed for adoption. At any subsequent time, the adoption agency is required to give notice to the birth parent when an adoption order is made or when the child is placed for adoption or when a placement ceases.

At any time after the expiration of 12 months from the making of a freeing order, a birth parent can apply to revoke the freeing order if no adoption order has been made in respect of the child and if the child does not then have his or her home with a person with whom he or she has been placed for adoption. On the making of such an application, the adoption agency may not place the child for adoption without the leave of the court. The revocation of a freeing order operates to extinguish the parental responsibility of the adoption agency and to revive any parental responsibility in any other person which had been extinguished by the freeing order.

Contact

There is no duty to promote contact between a child freed for adoption, or an adopted child, with his or her birth parents. It can be expected that the making of a freeing order will result in a speedy reduction in contact. Contact is likely to be an issue before the court making a freeing order and the court does have power to make an Article 8 order against the adoption agency in respect of the period between freeing and the making of an adoption order.

Post-adoption contact has increased significantly in recent years, perhaps as a consequence of children being older on average at the time of the making of an adoption order than was the case in previous years. There is some reason to suppose that for some older children with memories of a former family, continuing contact at a very limited level may be beneficial, but the test is always what is best for the child in his or her new family. One of the factors that is taken into account is the propensity of the birth parent to seek to disrupt the adoptive placement. The court does have a power to attach a condition as to contact to an adoption order or to make an Article 8 order, but it is rarely (if ever) exercised.

Adoption panels

Adoption agencies are required by the Adoption Agencies Regulations (Northern Ireland) 1989 to appoint an adoption panel, the functions of which are to consider reports provided by the adoption agency and make recommendations to the agency on the following matters:

- whether adoption is in the best interests of the child and, if so, whether a freeing application ought to be made;

- whether a prospective adopter is suitable to be an adoptive parent; and

- whether a prospective adopter would be a suitable adoptive parent for a particular child.

The recommendation must then be considered by the appropriate decision-maker for the adoption agency, which must give it proper consideration and then decide whether to accept or reject it. The panel and the decision-maker considering whether adoption is in the best interests of the child ought to provide an opportunity for the birth parents to make representations. A failure to follow the proper procedure may invalidate any subsequent freeing or adoption application.

Court procedure

Freeing and adoption applications may be brought in the High Court or the County Court. If there has been a care order application, subsequent freeing or adoption proceedings are usually brought in the court which made the care order – but note that the High Court has power to authorise some placements which the County Court cannot. Proceedings may be transferred from the County Court to the High Court and an appeal lies from the County Court to the High Court as from the ordinary civil jurisdiction of the County Court (Article 64 of the Adoption Order). All proceedings are held in private and are governed by Part IVA of the Family Proceedings Rules.

In freeing applications, the agency, as the applicant, has to lodge a statement of facts together with a report covering all the matters specified in Part 1 of Appendix 4 to the Rules. The parents and the child are parties. The statement of facts ought to be served on the parents but the confidential report is not. The parents may be able to obtain discovery of that part of the report that relates to them at a subsequent stage of the proceedings.

A NIGALA guardian ad litem[3] will be appointed whose duties include the investigation of whether any consent alleged has been properly and voluntarily obtained, whether any other parties need to be notified of the application and the investigation of the matters alleged both in the statement of facts and the confidential report. The guardian ad litem has to report to the court with a recommendation.

In adoption applications, the adopters are the applicants and the agency and the child are parties. The birth parents are not parties if the child has been freed for adoption. If the child has not been freed, then the parents are parties and the applicants have to prepare and serve a statement of facts showing why the parents' consent should be dispensed with. A NIGALA guardian ad litem will be appointed, as in the case of a freeing application, and that guardian has similar duties as in such an application. The agency is

3   Where there have been previous proceedings involving a guardian ad litem, the same guardian ad litem, if available, is usually appointed for the subsequent proceedings.

required to report to the court on the matters specified in Part I of Appendix 4 to the Rules.

The Adopted Children Register

The Registrar General for Northern Ireland keeps an Adopted Children Register which is open for public inspection and in which is recorded the date and country of birth of the adopted child, the name, surname and sex of the child, the name, surname and address of the adopters and the date of the adoption order and description of the court which made the order (Article 50 of the Adoption Order). The name and surname of the child registered will be the names specified in the adoption application by which the child is to be known.

An adopted person over the age of 18 may apply to the Registrar for such information as is necessary to enable such a person to obtain a certified copy of his or her birth certificate. If the person was adopted after 18 December 1987, the Registrar General has to inform the adopted person that counselling services are available. If that person chooses to receive counselling, then the Registrar General sends the relevant information to the agency or other body providing counselling. In the case of a person adopted before 18 December 1987, then the person must attend counselling and the information will be sent to the agency or other body providing counselling (Article 54 of the Adoption Order).

An adopted person under the age of 18, who intends to marry, may apply for and obtain from the Registrar General information as to whether or not it appears from the Registers that he or she and his or her proposed spouse may be within the prohibited degrees of relationship (Article 54(2) of the Adoption Order).

The Adoption Contact Register

The Registrar General maintains an Adoption Contact Register which is in two parts – one for adopted persons, and the other for relatives. An adopted person over the age of 18, whose records are kept by the Registrar General and who has obtained information from him or her under Article 54 of the Adoption Order or otherwise satisfies the Registrar General that he or she has such information as is necessary to obtain a certified copy of his or her birth certificate, may apply to be placed on the first part of the register. A relative, who is over the age of 18, of an adopted person whose records are kept by the Registrar General, who satisfies the Registrar General that he or she is a relative of an adopted person and that he or she has such information as is necessary to obtain a certified copy of the record of the adopted person's birth, may apply to have his or her name and address placed on the second part of the register. The Registrar General is obliged to transmit to an adopted person who is entered on the first part of the register the name and address of every relative of his or hers who is entered on the second part of the register (Article 54A of the Adoption Order).

Intercountry adoption

Intercountry adoption is a term used to describe the situation where someone from the UK wishes to adopt a child from overseas, or where someone from overseas wants to adopt a child from the UK.

The UK is a party to the 1993 Hague Convention on Protection of Children and Co-operation in respect of Intercountry Adoption, the text of which is scheduled to the Adoption (Intercountry Aspects) Act (Northern Ireland) 2001. The overall scheme of the Convention is that it is for the State of habitual residence of the child to determine whether the child is suitable for intercountry adoption and that all relevant consents and permissions have been given and remain maintained in place. It is for the State of the habitual residence of the adopters to determine whether they are suitable to adopt and, after the child has lawfully been brought to the State of the adopters, it is for the courts of that State to decide whether or not to make the adoption order. If an order is made, it is entitled to recognition in other signatory States. The Intercountry Adoption (Hague Convention) Regulations (Northern Ireland) 2003 specify the procedure to be followed in obtaining the relevant approvals and Part IVB of the Family Proceedings Rules specify and modify the adoption application procedure. If a child is being removed from Northern Ireland for the purposes of adoption outside the UK, the prospective adopters must obtain parental responsibility for the child from the court (Article 57 of the Adoption Order).

Adoption orders made in other parts of the UK are automatically recognised in Northern Ireland.

It is difficult to adopt a child from a non-Convention country. If the child is adopted in the child's country of origin, then difficulties may be encountered in terms of immigration control, unless the foreign adoption order is recognised in this country. It is prudent to liaise with and give notice of any foreign proceedings to the Home Office. If the order is recognised, then the child has a right of entry as the child of a UK national. It may be prudent to seek a declaration that a particular adoption order is entitled to recognition. A court asked to recognise an adoption order made in a non-Convention country will require expert evidence as to the process followed and the validity and effect of the order in the State in which it was made and will consider whether there are public policy grounds for refusing recognition.

It is an offence to bring a child into Northern Ireland for the purposes of adoption unless the requirements specified in Article 3 of the Adoption of Children from Overseas Regulations (Northern Ireland) 2002 are met. Assuming that those requirements are met, then the application is made and continues as if it were a domestic adoption application. At present, there are special difficulties in relation to bringing in children from Guatemala and Cambodia. Anyone contemplating a foreign adoption should seek specialised advice from an adoption agency or a solicitor (or both).

Further reading

Recourse may be had to the standard English textbooks on Family Law, Hershman and McFarlane on *Children Law and Practice* and *Butterworths Family Law Service*, but use with caution as the law may not be identical. On international aspects, *The International Family Law Practice*, by David Hodson *et al* (2012, now in its third edition) is essential, and on the rights of the child, *The Rights of the Child, Law and Practice* by Alistair MacDonald (2011) can be recommended. Both are published by Family Law.

In relation to Northern Ireland, the Courts Service website, www.courtsni. gov.uk, provides access not only to the COAC Best Practice Guide but also the *Guides to Case Management in Public and Private Law Proceedings* and the Allocation Guidance, and also all published High Court and Court of Appeal judgments. Statute Law is set out and annotated in my own *The Law of Adoption in Northern Ireland: The annotated legislation* (2002) and *The Law of Children in Northern Ireland: The annotated legislation* (2004), the latter having been written with Gemma Loughran. The annotations are now somewhat out of date but the text should be reliable.

Index